PERFIDIOUS
PROVERBS

AND OTHER POEMS

ALSO BY PHILIP APPLEMAN

POETRY:

Karma, Dharma, Pudding & Pie (Quantuck Lane Press / W. W. Norton & Co., 2009)
New and Selected Poems, 1956-1996 (University of Arkansas Press, 1996)
Let There Be Light (HarperCollins, 1991)
Darwin's Bestiary (Echo Press, 1986)
Darwin's Ark (Indiana University Press, 1984; 2nd ed., 2009)
Open Doorways (W. W. Norton & Co., 1976)
Summer Love and Surf (Vanderbilt University Press, 1968)
Kites on a Windy Day (Byron Press, England, 1967)

FICTION:

Apes and Angels (G. P. Putnam's Sons, 1989)
Shame the Devil (Crown Publishers, 1981)
In the Twelfth Year of the War (G. P. Putnam's Sons, 1970)

NONFICTION:

The Silent Explosion (Beacon Press, 1965)

EDITED WORKS:

Darwin (W. W. Norton & Co., 1970; 2001)
Malthus on Population (W. W. Norton & Co., 1976; 2004)
The Origin of Species (W. W. Norton & Co., 1975; 2002)
1859: Entering an Age of Crisis (Indiana University Press, 1959)
Victorian Studies (founding co-editor, 1957–1963)

PERFIDIOUS
PROVERBS
AND OTHER POEMS

A
SATIRICAL LOOK
AT THE BIBLE

PHILIP APPLEMAN

FOREWORD BY
DAN BARKER

Humanity
Books

an imprint of Prometheus Books
59 John Glenn Drive, Amherst, New York 14228-2119

Published 2011 by Humanity Books, an imprint of Prometheus Books

Inquiries should be addressed to
Humanity Books
59 John Glenn Drive
Amherst, New York 14228–2119
VOICE: 716–691–0133
FAX: 716–691–0137
WWW.PROMETHEUSBOOKS.COM

15 14 13   5 4 3

Library of Congress Cataloging-in-Publication Data

Appleman, Philip, 1926–
    Perfidious proverbs and other poems : a satirical look at the Bible / by Philip
Appleman ; foreword by Dan Barker.
        p. cm.
    ISBN 978–1–61614–385–5 (pbk. : alk. paper)
    ISBN 978–1–61614–440–1 (e-book)
    1. Verse satire, American. I. Title.

PS3551.P6P47 2011
811'.54—dc22   2011009843

Printed in the United States on acid-free paper

for Margie

*Let the words of my mouth
and the meditation of my heart
be acceptable in thy sight.*

CONTENTS

III. THE HOLY MEN

IV. LIVING WITH THE BIBLE

CONTENTS

V. SALVATION

ACKNOWLEDGMENTS

Written over a period of thirty years, these poems nevertheless have a unity of spirit and affirmation. They continue that ambitious effort, as old as the Greek and Roman poets, to instruct and please by means of satire.

I am grateful to the following publishers for permission to reprint poems that originally appeared in their volumes.

The University of Arkansas Press, *New and Selected Poems 1956-1996*
Quantuck Lane Press, *Karma, Dharma, Pudding & Pie*

Thanks are also due to the many magazines that had previously published these poems in their pages.

Lyrics to "This World Is Not My Home (I'm Just Passing Thru)" © Arr. Copyright 1936. Renewed 1964 by Albert E. Brumley & Sons/SESC (admin. by Clear Box Rights). All rights reserved. Used by permission.

FOREWORD

BY DAN BARKER

*Toss the Gideon bibles out of hotel rooms
and replace them with this book.*

Maybe it takes an artist to know one. I'm not talking about me being able to grasp Philip Appleman's remarkable work. I'm talking about Phil's ability to see the bible for what it is. It is all "art," after all: literature, poetry, and myth dressed up as historical fiction. When we were young and looking through the glass darkly, Phil and I both used to believe scripture was revealed truth. Now, as grown-up artists in our own way, we can see the bible for what it is: a fabulous fabrication.

When I took piano lessons as a young boy, the first real song I learned to play was a hymn:

WONDERFUL WORDS OF LIFE

> Sing them over again to me,
> Wonderful words of life,
> Let me more of their beauty see,
> Wonderful words of life;
> Words of life and beauty
> Teach me faith and duty.
> Beautiful words, wonderful words,
> Wonderful words of life.

My family was deeply fundamentalist and my growing musical skills were put to use for worship services and evangelistic outreach. During all those years of playing hymns, I was fascinated with how a message can be turned into art. How lyrics can be set to music. How the end result could be a seamless unit of inspiration, poetry, style, rhythm, and notes. But I took the message as a given. I would loudly play the piano as the congregation sang:

> There is a fountain filled with blood,
> Drawn from Immanuel's veins,
> And sinners plunged beneath that flood
> Lose all their guilty stains.

I didn't look too closely at those words, and even if I had, I wouldn't have recognized the ugliness. These were "wonderful words of life," as were all the verses in the bible. Jesus shed his blood for our sins, and what could be more amazing? To my family, the bible was the source of all truth

and beauty, the bedrock for morality and inspiration. It
gave us purpose in a meaningless world and hope for the
future.

As a Christian, I used to sing this simple, happy chorus
with gusto:

This world is not my home. I'm just a-passing
    through.
My treasures are laid up somewhere beyond the
    blue.
The angels beckon me from heaven's open door
And I can't feel at home in this world any more.

I suspect that is really bad poetry, but when I was
singing those lyrics, it was the heartfelt message that mat-
tered, not the quality of the art. Now that I am an atheist,
it is the same message that hits me, though today I cringe
at what I used to revere. (How can we *not* feel at home in our
own wonderful world?) This kind of "poetry"—all religious
art, I think—is so painted over with layers of doctrinal, cul-
tural, and subjective "meaning" that all perspective gets
lost, even when (maybe especially when) you disagree with
the sentiment. This is probably true of all art—we all have
our tastes—but religion stacks the deck. You don't have to
be a Muslim to appreciate Islamic architecture, but if you
are a Muslim, you are seeing that art, and the Koran, in a
completely different way, not as a free expression of human
yearning that may or may not be "beautiful" to anyone else,
but as a necessary part of the program. If it is from God, it
must be good.

I think that is what happens with the bible. It is known as "The Good Book," after all. After having been an evangelical minister for nineteen years, and now an atheist debater for twenty-five years, I imagine I have a pretty good grasp of what the bible says. "It ain't the parts of the Bible that I can't understand that bother me," Mark Twain said. "It is the parts that I do understand." But is the bible beautiful? Does it have any real poetry in it? I suppose that depends on your attitude and tastes, and maybe the tastes of the original readers were different from ours, but still, it is supposed to be a book of eternal truth for all ages. Mark Twain went on to say that the bible "has noble poetry in it, and some clever fables; and some blood-drenched history; and some good morals; and a wealth of obscenity; and upwards of a thousand lies." I agree with all of that except for the part about "noble poetry." I just can't see it. And not because I don't like what the bible says. I think my attitude toward the bible has been so papered over, so manhandled, that if there is any art there, I no longer have the perspective needed to make a fair judgment. I have lost the objectivity to be truly subjective.

Of course, I know that many of the biblical authors were writing poetry, or trying to. Even as a child I knew there was something different about the Psalms and Proverbs. Just look at them. They are structured in lines of roughly equal length. They use visual imagery, simile, metaphor, hyperbole, and so on. They often look like poems. I took a class in Hebrew Poetics and Wisdom Literature at my Christian college and learned that the Israelites composed their readings with certain styles that made things easier to remember, maybe because many were illiterate. Some of the poetry in the bible consists of the fact that each line begins with a different letter of the alphabet. There are some fascinating structures in parallel lines, synonymous and antithetical. This happens with lyrics all through history, so it must be deliberately poetic. Here is an example of a traditional blues form (with lyrics I just made up, which means this is the first and only time you will see them).

> That solitary whistle comes callin' down the track.
> That solitary whistle comes callin' down the track.
> There ain't no way to answer, unless you take me
>   back.

This is not unlike what happens in many of the psalms, proverbs, songs, and lamentations, with the second line rephrasing or supporting the first. Look at the Song of Solomon 1:15-16:

> How beautiful you are, my darling,
> How beautiful you are!
> Your eyes are like doves.
> How handsome you are, my beloved,
> And so pleasant!
> Indeed, our couch is luxuriant!

I don't know if that is great poetry, but it is definitely a love poem. (Of course, every lover's poem is great to the lover, if not to the lovee.) Look at the famous Isaiah 2:4, where the second line restates the first:

And they shall beat their swords into plowshares,
And their spears into pruninghooks:
Nation shall not lift up sword against nation,
Neither shall they learn war any more.

So, yes, there is poetry in the bible, I have to admit.
Some of it resonates today, and some does not. But is it good
poetry? "Trusting your heart may not be awfully bright,"
Philip Appleman writes, "But trusting Proverbs is an idiot's
delight."
Look at Psalm 137:8, 9:

O daughter of Babylon, who art to be
    destroyed;
Happy shall he be, that rewardeth thee as thou
    hast served us.
Happy shall he be, that taketh and dasheth thy
    little ones against the stones.

This is like an upside-down blues, where the last line,
not the first, is restated. Structurally, this is clearly poetry.
But are these "wonderful words of life"?
One of my friends at Azusa Pacific College was Leo
Depalma, who also studied for the ministry. We took
second-year Greek together and were the only two students
in the class. One day while Leo and I were talking outside
the cafeteria, he opened the bible and asked me to read
Psalm 137:9. I read it out loud: "Happy shall he be, that
taketh and dasheth thy little ones against the stones."
"What do you think of that?" he asked.

"What do you mean?" I replied.

"Should we be happy to kill innocent babies?"

"No," I answered with confidence. "This is not talking about real babies."

"Oh? What is it talking about?"

"The little babies in this verse," I brilliantly improvised, "represent the little sins in your life that you don't want to give up. They are precious creatures that we hold dear, like drinking or smoking or cheating on taxes or gambling or parties. But to be a true Christian, you have to dash those darling temptations against the rocks," I exulted. That would make a great sermon, I thought. Leo shook his head, closed the bible, and said nothing. (Leo, if you are reading this, I'm so sorry! It astonishes me to realize that I did not see what you were seeing.)

Notice that those "wonderful words of death" of Psalm 137:9 don't say that believers might regretfully have to take drastic action that results in unfortunate collateral damage during war time, for a greater cause. It says believers should be happy (or "blessed," in some translations) to kill the innocent infants of nonbelievers.

I can see that most of the bible is not to be admired, not poetically or morally. Why did I ever think they were "wonderful words"? Maybe Leo was not in the place to do it, but why didn't someone come up to me and turn my face back to those verses and say, "Open your eyes! Is this good? Look at what the bible is really saying." Well, it wouldn't have worked. I wasn't a grownup yet.

Part of being an adult is the ability to take a different point of view. Poetry doesn't have to have a point, but it does need a point of view. Look at what Phil does in this book. He points with his eyes. We know that the human species has very large sclera—the white part of the eyes—in order to communicate visually and silently: "Look over there." Phil has pulled our glance away from the normal path, not away from the bible, but deeper into it. Why should the authors speak for the characters? Especially authors with a religious agenda? Why not let the characters speak for themselves? If you trust the official Catholic Church, Mother Teresa was a saint; but it you read Mother Teresa's own words, her own thoughts were nothing like the hagiography of the Vatican's PR department. She had doubts. She admitted that her real life was nothing like the character she was being forced to play in someone else's narrative. "The place of God in my soul is blank," she confessed to a friend. What if we could interrogate the biblical characters directly to see if they were accurately portrayed?

Imagine if Mary, the mother of Jesus, could speak for herself. Unless we find a trove of ancient affidavits, the only way we can do that today is through fiction. It's all fiction anyway: the biblical authors were, after all, authors. If their compositions count as truth, then so do Phil's—but his are infinitely more fun to read. And when they are not intended to be fun, they are powerful. (I actually read "Gertrude" out loud during a public debate. It is that powerful.) Like the biblical authors, Phil has a point of view, but he is admitting it openly by deliberately yanking our perspective to the side: a point of view with a point of view.

"Mary" is one of the most incredible poems I have ever read. "Not exactly what you'd want for your son, is it?"

Between the lines, behind the lines, and the lines themselves all shift the camera angle from the sham orthodox cry for miracles to focus on the human story behind the scenes.

Toss the Gideon bibles out of hotel rooms and replace them with this book!

Most of the poems here—from "Days" to "Daisies"—are freely structured, but a few have a regular rhythm, and Phil has allowed me to set some of them to music. You can hear "God's Grandeur" on the *Friendly Neighborhood Atheist* CD, and "Fleas" on *Beware of Dogma* (I didn't compose that music, of course), as well as "Summers of Love" (not in this book). Two more of Phil's poems, "In a Dark Time" and "Intelligent Design?" (not in this book) will appear on my next CD. You can listen to Phil himself, with his wife, Marjorie, reciting a version of "Noah" on *Beware of Dogma*, backed up by a wailing Semitic clarinet. When they performed that one live before the Freedom From Religion Foundation convention in San Diego, the entire audience was transfixed. The punch line, as you will see, is not just funny, but profound.

I long ago lost the gift of prophecy, but I will make a secular prediction here: many of the lines in this book are destined for the quote books. You will find your own, but here are some of my favorites:

"Maybe we're all exactly like gods. And maybe that's our really original sin."

"This is the only real revelation—that God is only a trick with mirrors, our dark reflection in a glass."

"God must have a weird sense of values, and if there's a

Judgment Day, as some folks think, He's going to have a lot to answer for."

JUDAS: "Well, with or without those thirty pieces of silver, it's a wonder that none of the others crossed him first."

"Why can't pious people just be moral?"

HEAVEN: "The big apartheid in the sky."

I can't end without singing highest praise for my favorite, "Gathering at the River." I have no trouble at all seeing that this is great poetry. It is so good that it should *not* be set to music—just as it would be a huge mistake to put lyrics to Gershwin's "Rhapsody in Blue." I read this one twice in a row, and keep going back to it, like a song you want to hear again and again.

> ". . . Imagine,
> not eons of boredom or pain,
> but honest earth-to-earth;
> and when our bodies rise again,
> they will be wildflowers, then rabbits,
> then wolves, singing a perfect love
> to the beautiful, meaningless moon."

I agree with Phil that there is no meaning of life, and that is what makes it so precious. Life is its own reward: a song that doesn't need words. But the fact that there is no meaning of life does not mean there is no meaning *in* life. As long as there is such beauty to create and admire—as long as we have Phil Appleman's wonderful words—there is immense meaning in life.

INTRODUCTION

C hildhood is a time of wondrous tales: Snow White and the dwarfs, Daniel and the lions; Santa at the Pole, Jonah in the whale; Peter Pan flying, Jesus walking on water; and so on, and on, and on.

As the years creep by, we are slowly weaned away from some of those childhood wonders. No, Santa won't be coming down the chimney tonight; no, the tooth fairy won't be checking your pillow. And yet some of the wonders survive: the talking snake still speaks, the water-walking continues, bread goes on magically multiplying itself. As the difficult transition to adulthood moves ahead, we are gradually socialized away from magic dragons and wonderlands, but are encouraged to remain faithful to the ancient hero with his invincible slingshot, to a primitive wooden boat that could float every species of animal on earth, to a virgin somehow managing to gestate a baby.

Of course there is no mystery about why some fables survive while others slip away; it is simply because some have institutional support, and others don't. And the reason for that continuing support is that it's mutual: churches support myths because myths support churches. And what the churches (and mosques and synagogues) promote, along with their pious protestations, is a self-serving myopia that is all too often socially destructive and sometimes devastating: the wars of religion, around the world and down through the ages, have caused massive human loss and human misery, which continues unabated today.

Intelligent and well-meaning people have argued for centuries against the fatal attraction of foolishness, but their efforts have been largely unproductive, partly because many people seem impervious to rational discussion. So perhaps satire is our most effective way of lighting candles in the darkness and communicating effectively to those who are immune to reason. That is, at any rate, the hope, and the rationale, of this book.

P.A.

I.

THE CREATOR

THE CREATOR
DAYS ONE THROUGH SIX, ETC.

You keep on asking me that—
"Which day was the hardest?"
Blockheads! They were *all* hard—
And of course, since I'm omnipotent,
They were all easy.
It was Chaos, to begin with. Can you imagine
Primeval Chaos? Of course you can't.
How long had it been swirling around out there?
Forever.
How long had I been there?
Longer than that.
It was a mess, that's what it was. Chaos is
Rocky. Fuzzy. Slippery. Prickly.
As scraggly and obstreperous as the endless behind
of an infinite jackass. Shove on it anywhere,
it gives, then slips in behind you,
like smog, like lava, like slag.
I'm telling you, chaos is—*chaotic.*
You see what I was up against. Who
could make a world out of that muck?
I could, that's who—land
from water, light from dark, and so on.
It might seem like a piece of cake
now that it's done, but
back then, without a blueprint,
without a set of instructions, without a committee,
could *you* have created a *firmament?*

Of course there were bugs in the process,
grit in the gears, blips, bloopers—
bringing forth grass and trees on Day Three
and not making sunlight until Day Four, that,
I must say, wasn't my best move.
And making the animals and vegetables before
there was any rain whatsoever—well,
anyone can have a bad day.
Even Adam, as it turned out, wasn't such a great
idea—those shifty eyes, the alibis,
blaming things on his wife—I mean,
it set a bad example. How could he
expect that little toddler, Cain,
to learn correct family values
with a role model like him?
And then there was the nasty squabble
over the beasts and birds.
OK, I admit I told Adam
to name them, but—Platypus?
Aardvark? Hippopotamus?
Let me make one thing perfectly clear—
he didn't get that gibberish from *Me*.
No, I don't need a planet to fall on Me,
I know something about subtext.
He did it to irritate Me, just plain
spite—and did I need the aggravation?
Well, as you know, things went from bad
to worse, from begat to begat,
father to son, the evil fruit
of all that early bile. So next

there was narcissism, then bigotry,
then jealousy, rage, *vengeance!*
And finally I realized, the spawn of Adam
had become exactly like—Me.

No Deity with any self-respect
would tolerate that kind
of competition, so what could I do?
I killed them all, that's what!
Just as the Good Book says,
I drowned man, woman, and child, like
so many cats. Oh, I saved a few
for restocking, Noah and his crew,
the best of the lot, I thought. But
now you're back to your old tricks again,
just about due for another good ducking,
or maybe a giant barbecue.
And I'm warning you, if I have to do it again,
there won't be any survivors, not even
a cockroach! Then,
for the first time since it was Primeval
Chaos, the world will be perfect—
nobody in it but Me.

ON THE SEVENTH DAY

I rested, and thought it over.
What was it *for*, then, after all—
that cosmic labor,
the lumbering stars, the planets,
earth, and voluptuous Eden—and yes,
My one big gamble: Adam, Eve,
the only things I couldn't be quite sure of.

And yet of course I *was* sure, had
fondled the whole thing in My lonely mind
since—well, forever—all
programmed there, ready
to play itself out just as I knew
it had to: the serpent, the fall,
the flaming sword, the steady slide into sin,
the flood . . .

So *why*, I asked Myself again,
what, after all, was the *point*? Just think
of all that bother—and now the obligation
of having to throw a fuss every time
I noticed a measly venial sin, some
small-time swindle—as if it made
a difference in the scheme of things.

Resting there, in that post-
partum depression—after all the planning,
the tough decisions, the perfect

execution—I knew
I knew the answer,
had to know it: I knew I was omniscient.
That's one of the things you know
when you're omniscient.
So had it been just the loneliness?
God knows (I thought) it's lonely at the top.
And yet . . .

Why, of course: it was the boredom,
the unbearable monotony
of endless time and empty space, and
angels—
everywhere I looked, a skyful of nothing
but angels and archangels, cherubim
and seraphim, rank upon rank, all
perfect. And virtuous. And dull.
Not even Satan and his little band
of hooligans had amused Me much,
the battle so pitifully short, so predictable,
the road to hell paved
with predestination. No,
if being God was going to be worth it all,
if I was going to get any fun
out of the job, I needed
something permanent, but evanescent,
something negligible, but outrageous.
I needed that big bang, of course,
and dying suns,
swirling gases, planets with protozoa,

worms, frogs, monkeys—but
I also needed
something—someone—special, someone
capable of understanding how cleverly
I'd stacked the deck—capable of knowing
how My omniscient
omnipotence smothered
justice, and mercy, and love—capable
of tragedy.
So at the last hour, on the last day,
I made up My mind: *do* it,
and call it Man, or Woman, or, why not,
create both of them, and let them
help each other
die.

I had to smile, remembering Satan,
down there now in that eternal fire.
Hell already existed, after all—so
let Man and Woman enter.

GOD'S GRANDEUR

God will laugh at the trial of the innocent.
—Job, 9:23

When they hunger and thirst, and I send down a
    famine,
When they pray for the sun, and I drown them
    with rain,
And they beg me for reasons, my only reply is:
I never apologize, never explain.

When the Angel of Death is a black wind around
    them
And children are dying in terrible pain,
Then they burn little candles in churches, but still
I never apologize, never explain.

When the Christians kill Jews, and Jews kill the
    Muslims,
And Muslims kill writers they think are profane,
They clamor for peace, or for reasons, at least,
But I never apologize, never explain.

When they wail about murder and torture and
    rape,
When unlucky Abel complains about Cain,
And they ask me just why I had planned it like
    this,
I never apologize, never explain.

Of course, if they're smart, they can figure it out—
The best of all reasons is perfectly plain.
It's because I just happen to like it this way—
So I never apologize, never explain.

II.

THE CREATED

EVE

Clever, he was, so slick
he could weave words into sunshine.
When he murmured another refrain
of that shimmering promise, "You
shall be as gods," something with wings
whispered back in my heart,
and I crunched the apple—a taste so good
I just had to share it with Adam,
and all of a sudden
we were naked.
Oh, yes, we were nude before, but now,
grabbing for fig leaves, we knew
that we knew too much, just as the slippery
serpent said—so we crouched all day
under the rhododendrons, trembling
at something bleak and windswept in our bellies
that soon we'd learn to call by its right name:
fear.
God was furious with the snake
and hacked off his legs on the spot
And for us
it was thorns and thistles,
sweat of the brow, dust
to dust returning. In that sizzling
skyful of spite whirled
the whole black storm of the future:
the flint knife in Abel's heart,
the incest that swelled us into a tribe,

a nation, and
brought us all, like driven lambs,
straight to His flood.
I blamed it on human nature, even then,
when there were only two humans around,
and if human nature was a mistake,
whose mistake was it? *I didn't ask
to be cursed with curiosity, I only wanted
the apple,*
and of course that promise—to be
like gods. But then,
maybe we are like gods.
Maybe we're all exactly like gods.
And maybe that's our really original
sin.

NOAH

Seed of Methuselah,
already six hundred years old,
more than a little weary
from all that virtuous living—then
a finger out of the clouds points down at him,
and a Voice full of blood and bones
bullies the stony hillsides:
"Make thee an ark of gopher wood . . ."
Details follow, in that same
bossy baritone: "The boat shall be
four hundred fifty feet long
seventy-five feet wide
three decks
one window
one door."

And then
the Voice tells him why.

His sons, Shem, Ham, and Japheth, just
cannot handle this news.
"He's going to drown them all?" Japheth whispers,
"Every last woman and child? What for?"
Noah's mind is not what it used to be; lately
it strays like a last lamb, his ancient voice
a bleat: "Ahh—
wickedness, I think that's
what He said—yes, wickedness."

Too vague for Japheth: "But wicked how? I mean,
what are the charges?"
The old brow wrinkles again. "Evil, that's
what He said. Corruption. Violence."
"Violence! What do you call
this killer flood? He's going to murder
the lot of them, just
for making a few mistakes? For being—human?"
Now Japheth is really riled. Being the youngest,
he still has a lot of drinking pals around—
Enos and Jared, and sexy Adah
and his pretty young neighbor,
Zillah—together they'd put away
many a goatskin of red wine
under the big desert stars. Besides,
being a kid, a mere ninety years old,
he still likes to stump his father
with embarrassing questions. "Listen,
Dad, I thought you said He
was omniscient—well, then,
wouldn't He have foreseen all this? And if He did,
why did He make us the way we are
in the first place?"

"Ours not to reason why," says Shem, the firstborn
and something of a prig. "Ours but to build the
    ark."
"That's another thing," Japheth scowls. "Just
what is an ark? I mean,
we're desert people, after all—nomads,

living out here in this miserable dry scrub
with our smelly goats and camels—
I never saw a boat in my life."
"I saw one once," Noah quavers,
"but I don't remember it very well,
that was four hundred years ago—
or was it five, let's see . . ."
"It can't be that hard," says Ham,
always the practical one. "An ordinary boat,
we'll mock one up. You need a keel, that's it,
you begin with a keel of gopher wood,
and the rest is easy—ribs, then planks,
pitch, decking. Don't worry, Dad,
I'll handle it."

So finally they have themselves an ark,
and God says, "Good work, Noah, now
get the animals—clean beasts, seven of a kind,
unclean, just two, but make sure
they're male and female, you got that straight?
And hurry it up, so I can get
the drowning started."
Noah was hoping the animals
would be easy, but Japheth
knows better. "Dad,
did He say *every* animal?"
"Every animal," Noah repeats,
quoting Authority. "Every living thing
of all flesh—fowl,
cattle, creeping things. Plus
food enough for a year."

Think of it—they're living out there
in that gritty wilderness, and all of a sudden
they're supposed to come up with two elephants.
Or is it more?
"Shem," Japheth calls. "Is the elephant
a clean or an unclean animal?
If it's clean, that means seven of them
And the ark is in trouble. And how
about rhinos? And hippos? What do we do
about the dinosaurs? How do we get a brontosaurus
up the gangplank? Japheth
loves raising problems that Noah
hasn't thought of at all. "Pandas—kids
love pandas, we can't let them die out,
but how do we get two of them here
in a hurry, all the way from China?
And, oh, by the way, Dad,
how are we going to keep the lions
away from the lambs?"

It's not just a headache; it's a nightmare.
Just think of poor Ham, after all of his angst
and sweat getting the ark assembled, and then
having to trudge off to the Congo and the Amazon
to round up all those tricky
long-tailed leapers, there in the jungle greenery—
gibbons, orangutans, gorillas, baboons, chimps,
howler monkeys, spider monkeys, squirrel
       monkeys,
capuchins, mandrills, tamarins . . .

And Shem, dutiful Shem, in charge
of the other mammals—the giraffes,
the horses, zebras, quaggas, tapirs, bison,
the pumas, bears, shrews, raccoons, weasels,
skunks, mink, badgers, otters, hyenas,
the rats, bats, rabbits, chipmunks, beavers—
thousands of species of mammals . . .

And Japheth out there on the cliffs and treetops
trying to snare the birds—the eagles,
condors, hawks, buzzards, vultures, and every
winged beauty in the rain forests—and bring them
    back,
chattering, twittering, fluttering around
on the top deck, thousands upon thousands
of hyperkinetic birds . . .

Two by two
they come strolling through:
antelope, buffalo, camel, dog,
egret, ferret, gopher, frog,
quail and wombat, sheep and goose,
turtle, nuthatch, ostrich, moose,
ibex, jackal, kiwi, lark,
two by two they board the ark.

Well, it's pretty clear, isn't it,
that there's a space problem here: a boat
only four hundred fifty feet long, already
buzzing and bleating and squeaking and mooing

and grunting and mewing and hissing and cooing
and croaking and roaring and peeping and howling
and chirping and snarling and clucking and
    growling—
and the crocodiles aren't back from the Nile
yet, or the iguanas from the islands,
or the kangaroos or koalas, or
the pythons or boas or cotton-mouth moccasins
or the thirty different species of rattlesnake
or the tortoises, salamanders, centipedes, toads . . .

It takes some doing, all that,
but Ham comes back with them.
And wouldn't you know,
it's Japheth who opens up, so to speak,
the can of worms. "Dad, there are thousands
of species of worms! Who's
going digging for them? And oh, yes,
how about the insects?"
"Insects!" Shem rebels at last,
"Dad, do we have to save *insects*?" Noah,
faithful servant, quotes the Word:
"Every living thing."
"But Dad, the cockroaches?"
Noah has all the best instincts
of a minor bureaucrat—he
is only following orders—the roaches
go aboard.

Japheth ticks away at his roster. "So far
we've got dragonflies, damselflies, locusts, and
    aphids,
grasshoppers, mantises, crickets, and termites . . .
Wait a minute—termites?
We're going to save termites, in a wooden boat?"
But Japheth knows that arguing with Noah
is like driving a nail into chicken soup. He shrugs
and carries on. "We've got lice,
beetles—God knows how many beetles.
We've got bedbugs, cooties, gnats, and midges,
horseflies, sawflies, bottleflies, fireflies.
We've got ants, bees, wasps, hornets—
can you imagine what it's going to be like
cooped up with *them* for a whole year?
But Dad, we haven't even scratched the surface.
There must be a million species
of insects out there.
Even if we unload all the other animals,
the insects alone will sink the ark!"

Ah, but the ark was not floating on fact,
it was floating on faith—that is to say,
on fiction. And in fiction, the insects
went aboard—*and* a year's supply
of hay for the elephants, a year's bananas
for the monkeys, and so on.
"Well, that's that," Japheth says,
"but you still haven't answered my question—
what will the meat-eaters eat?"

"We'll cross that bridge when we come to it,"
Noah replies, in history's
least appropriate trope,
"All aboard, now, it's starting
to sprinkle."

So the fountains of the great deep
were broken up, and the windows of heaven
        opened,
and the rain was upon the earth
forty days and forty nights,
and the ark was lifted up
and went upon the face of the waters—
and the drowning began.
Noah pretended not to know,
And so did Shem and Ham, so
it was only Japheth who keened
for Enos and Jared, still out there
somewhere, and for Adah and beautiful Zillah.
He was the first to peek
out of the one small window, and yes,
there it was, just the way fear
had been painting it on his eyelids ever since
that divine command: people fighting
for high ground, crazed beasts goring
and gnashing, serpents dangling from trees.
Finally, Shem, Ham, and Noah
and the four nameless wives
couldn't resist—they looked out the window, too,
and watched their friends

hugging in love and panic until
they all went under. Japheth caught
one final glimpse, and of course it had to be Zillah,
holding her baby over her head
till the water rolled over her
and she sank, and the baby
splashed a little, and then
there was silence upon the waters,
and God was well pleased.
They all turned away from the window, Noah
and his sons and the weeping women,
and no one would look into anyone's eyes
for many days.

Twelve hard months that strange menagerie lived
in the ark, the sixteen thousand hungry birds
lusting for the two million insects,
and the twelve thousand snakes and lizards
nipping at the seven thousand mammals,
and everyone slipping and sliding around
on the sixty-four thousand worms
and the one hundred thousand spiders—
and Noah driving everyone buggy, repeating
every morning, as if he'd just thought of it,
"Well, we're all in the same boat."
It was a long, long year
for those weary men and their bedraggled wives,
feeding the gerbils and hamsters, cleaning
the thousands of cages, keeping the jaguars
away from the gazelles, the grizzlies away

from the cottontails—everything aboard, after all,
was an endangered species.
But finally the waters subsided,
the dove fluttered off and never returned,
the gangplank slid down to Ararat,
and the animals scrambled out to the muddy,
corpse-ridden earth.

And Noah, burning a lamb on his altar
under that mocking rainbow, cannot forget
that he rescued the snakes and spiders, but
he let Enoch and Jubal
and Cainan and Lamech and
their wives and innocent children
go to a soggy grave.
And Noah knows, in his tired bones,
that now he will have to be fruitful once more,
and multiply and replenish the earth
with a pure new race of people who
would never, *never* sin again,
for if they did,
all that killing would be for nothing,
a terrible embarrassment
to God.

SARAH

You remember me,
the tough-luck wife of Abraham—
a beauty, they called me
in the old days in Egypt, a flower
fit for Pharaohs. But now
I'm just a gray granny who pesters you
with the tales they used to tell
around the evening fire . . .

The story goes
that after the great flood drained away—
drained away to *where*, I always wondered—
then Noah came limping down the gangplank,
feeling older than old, downright ante-
diluvian, and looked around, left and right.
Everywhere he looked
he saw nothing with those cloudy eyes
but landscapes of corpses and skeletons.
So who could blame him if he drank too much
and sprawled around in the buff all day? I mean,
given that heavy load of guilt,
friends and neighbors gone to mushy death,
wouldn't you?
Anyway, that's all the poor guy did
For over three hundred years until,
just twenty candles shy of Methuselah's record,
he finally turned up his toes.
Meanwhile, Shem, Ham, and Japheth

and their anonymous wives were going at it
day and night, getting the begetting going
again, the way the Lord commanded. Sure enough,
Shem—a hundred years old after the flood—
Shem begat a son he named
Arphaxad.
In due time
Arphaxad begat Salah
who begat Eber
who begat Peleg—
and so it went, for another hundred years,
until Terah begat my husband, Abram,
and Abram's brother, the father of Lot.

When he came to itchy manhood, Abram
looked upon me with favor—I
was an eyeful in those days, remember—and
he made me his wife.
We all moved off to Canaan,
Abram in the country to the west, Lot near a more
sophisticated town called Sodom.
And we prospered.
But then
God changed Abram's name to Abraham,
and told him, "Look, I've heard
that Sodom over there is a swamp of perversion,
Gomorrah, too. If that's really true . . ."

We both knew God well enough to see
where this was heading.

We still remembered the flood, not
that long ago, after all.
We knew that when God
gets into a rage, He smites
everything in sight, rain falling
on the just and the unjust. Then
Abraham thought of his nephew Lot,
over by Sodom,
so before God gets ten steps away,
he runs after Him, shouting,
"Lord! Lord! Wait a minute! How about
all the good folks over there? Family men,
chaste women, keepers of the Sabbath,
salt of the earth—
are you going to blast them right along
with the perverts? Listen,
there might be, say, fifty saints
in that poor town.
Wouldn't you save it, for their sakes?"
Oh, that was nervy enough, but then
I thought I'd collapse
when Abraham turns the screw again:
"Shall not . . ." he begins—I can see his legs
quivering as he says it—"Shall not
the judge of all the earth
do right?"

When I dare to look,
they're still nose to nose,
my poor Abe quaking like a weed in a windstorm,

but firm in his nephew's cause,
and God, gone white as a thunderhead, but so far
not losing His temper the way He always did
down in Egypt, blazing away
at everything that moved.
Pretty soon He nods a bit,
like a camel trader who's just been outwitted,
and mutters, "All right, Abraham, .
you find me fifty diamonds
in that dirt, and I'll back off."
He turns to go, and finally
I can breathe again. But then
Abraham calls out,
"God! Yahweh! Listen! I'm a nothing,
I'm the dirt under your sandals,
I'm the ashes from your campfire,
I'm a pest, forgive me for asking,
I shouldn't mention it—but suppose,
just suppose I come up short by five, just five short,
what then, would you burn the place for five?"
God is a little quicker this time—
you know how it is, once you have
a deal cooking, things go easier—
and He says, gritting His teeth a little,
All right, Abraham, Patriarch,
Father of My Nation, for forty-five
I'll save the slimy place."
But before I can relax,
Abe blurts out, not even pretending
to grovel, "How about forty?"

God comes right back,
"OK, forty,
forty's OK,"
and turns on His heel.

So this time when Abraham calls again, I figure
it's all up with us, he's gone too far,
you can't haggle like this, not
with the Lord Himself, not even
in the Middle East. But Abraham
goes all oily: "God, please, don't get mad,
but say now—how about thirty?"
God doesn't even turn around. "Thirty. Done."
And Abe: "Twenty? Twenty righteous souls,
twenty virtuous, circumcised, ram-killing,
bullock-burning, tithe-paying citizens
who love the Lord?"
God is slouching down our front path,
kicking stones. I can barely hear
His gruff voice. "All right. Agreed.
It's a deal."

And I pray to myself—quit
while you're still ahead, Abraham! This
is the Lord of flood and plague,
the jealous God, God of the flaming sword,
the God of pestilence, the Angel of Death,
you're playing with fire, enough, *enough!*

But he has to do it one more time,
old goat-seller, bargain-hunter,

carpet-buyer, his whole life an endless
flea market, it must have come over him
like a nervous tic, irresistible, his voice
full of the fever of wheeling and dealing, and of
    course
the unbearable fear of losing it all—
after so many years I recognize
the symptoms. *"God!"* he shouts.
My stomach cramps up, my eyes squeeze shut,
waiting for the end. "God,
don't get mad, I swear
this is the last time,
but wait—*how about ten?"*
And I catch the quick crackle of lightning,
the stench of burning flesh . . .
But no, it's only God's voice,
fading in the distance: "I will not
destroy it for ten's sake."

So that, at last, is that. Abraham
is still standing there in our gravel path,
sweat staining his summer robes.
I run to him and hug him, glad
for the little cakes I baked for God that morning,
glad for the fatted calf we killed
and fed Him, knowing that full bellies
make good tempers. But Abe is all unstrung
by the terrible chance he's taken.
As I lead him back to the tent like a cripple,
he mumbles again and again, how hard it is

to make the judge of all the earth
do right.

You can guess what happened next.
There hadn't even been a handshake,
let alone a contract, and like they say
out here in the Holy Land, a verbal deal
isn't worth the parchment it's written on.
So to make a long story short,
when Lot heard that God was reneging,
he got out of Sodom fast,
taking his wife and daughters
up to the mountains, an angel warning them
not to look back on that holy
holocaust. But when the red-hot coals
winged over Sodom, and the fire
began falling from heaven, Lot's wife
just *had* to check it out, just for a minute. And God,
with that sense of humor He's famous for,
turned her into a pillar of salt, ha-ha.
Then Lot and his two sexy daughters
dug into a cave, where they all got drunk,
and there, in the godly stink of brimstone, enjoyed
a little incest, and the two girls
both gave birth to sons. Or brothers, depending
on how you look at it. And Lot had sons,
or grandsons, suit yourself, and that's
all I'm going to say about that family. I mean,
if you put this in a book,
nobody in his right mind would believe it.

But whenever I think of Sodom . . . Well,
what had those people done that was so bad,
anyway—some dice and booze,
some frisky girls, willing boys,
a little fooling around—I know
it's not exactly orthodox, but
to kill them all? To peel
the cooked flesh off those one-year-olds,
just learning their first words?
All I can say is,
God must have a weird set of values,
and if there's a Judgment Day,
as some folks think,
He's going to have a lot to answer for.

BILDAD

I know what they're saying
under their breath, behind my back,
men in the sweaty bazaar,
women at the well near sundown. "He's
a tent flap in the wind," they're saying.
"His knots have come loose. Bildad
can't walk and count goats at the same time."
Well, let them talk. We knew
what we were doing, Zophar,
Eliphaz, and I, we knew our minds,
our duty, our holy obligation.
So we sat with Job for seven days
and seven nights, for his own good.
What, after all,
was in it for us but righteousness,
piety, the love of God—a God as good
and kind and loving and just
as *we* were?

Job was our friend, so when we heard
how his thousands of sheep and camels and oxen
were carried off, his children slaughtered,
servants put to the sword,
his body blistered with boils,
and only his wife still alive
to scald him with her constant
"Curse God and die"—
why naturally we had to come and sit with him,

there in the ashes. He was a mess,
frankly—those festering sores,
his head shaved ragged, his robe in tatters,
and he smelled like a day-old fish—
but what's all that among friends?

We wanted to let him talk first,
so we waited. And waited.
After those seven long days he finally spoke:
"God breaks me like a tempest.
He wounds me without cause."

That's when our sacred mission began:
"Job, you've got it all wrong,
God doesn't punish the innocent.
Think, deep in your heart,
where you've sinned, but don't
blame the Lord."
That shook him up, his eyes
darting around at us like someone
looking for a way to run.
"But I *am* innocent!" he whined.
We all had to smile,
and he jabbered on, "The arrows of the Almighty
are poisoning me. Let the day perish
when I was born . . ."
We shut him off, before his self-pity
stuck to our skin like pitch.
"Job! A hypocrite's hope
is a spiderweb, a flower in the withering sun,

its roots in stone—but the good Lord
will not cast away a perfect man."

Oh, we had him all right,
locked in logic.
He twisted and turned, and hassled us
with more of his graveyard metaphor:
"Man that is born of woman," he wailed,
"cometh forth like a flower
and is cut down. Man dieth
and riseth not. If God's scourge
kills the innocent, He
will sit there and laugh . . ."

We stopped him short. "Job,
the light of the wicked
shall be put out, the hypocrite
perish, the meat in his bowels
turned to gall, he shall vomit up
his ill-gotten riches,
he shall suck the poison of asps, burn
fire in his private places. So
confess—you must have stripped
the naked of their clothing,
sent widows away empty-handed, broken
the arms of orphans. Almighty God
is just. Confess. *Confess*."

I tell you we had him. Our syllogism
was airtight: since God is just,

He cannot torment
an innocent man;
the conclusion was as clear
as a desert sky. Job
must be guilty.

But then God opened His mouth
and in a whirlwind of rage
blasted our beautiful logic.
Out of a dust storm it came, that booming
irrelevance: "Where were you   .
when I made the earth, the stars,
the sea? Do you know the breadth of the world,
the treasures of the snow?
Out of whose womb comes the ice?
Can you send down the lightning?"
And more of the same, all meaning—
Why do you bother Me with your sniveling,
you insignificant maggot?
"Will you condemn Me," roared
the grimy whirlwind, "so you can be righteous?"

Some scene, isn't it? There we are,
making sense of things, putting Job in his place,
proving the neat connection between
crime and punishment—and just as our triumph
burns in Job's bewildered eyes,
God horns in with that scandalous
non sequitur. "No," He says,
"You don't suffer because you sin.
You suffer because I say so."

And Job, humble at last in spirit
as he already was in body, groveled in dirt:
"I abhor myself, Lord—I repent
in dust and ashes."

That did it. God
was finally satisfied, and Job
got his reward: his camels back,
doubled, his sheep and oxen, too, and now
his wife is pregnant, a brand-new bundle
on its way. As I always say,
toadying is good for business. Still,
this whole affair
was just cosmic whimsy, and
who needs it? That's why I don't care
when the locals whisper behind my back
and call me crazy.
But I've got children, too. Who's
going to explain this
celestial farce
to them? All I can hope now is
that Job will be utterly forgotten, and
that God's awful pronouncement
will be buried in Job's grave.
It's hard enough to bring up a family
in these troubled times without admitting
that almighty God has the morals
of a Babylonian butcher.

DAVID

After my smooth stone crushed
his head, I hacked at the throat
with his own great sword
and dragged back my ugly trophy,
oozing blood. Then
came the rout and the sexy slaughter—
I gave the guts of Philistine boys
to the buzzards and beasts
of the earth. Our women
sang in the streets, "O Saul
has slain his thousands, but David
his tens of thousands."
    I am David, I am mighty,
      and behold, the Lord is with me.

For my promised wife Michal, King Saul
demanded the foreskins of
one hundred Gentiles. I made instead
two hundred weeping widows
and cast those gory flaps
at the feet of the king, amid praises.
And God said, "I will deliver all
the Philistines into thy hands."
So I smote them hip and thigh,
and we spitted every man,
and buried our tools and our knives
in the soft flesh of their women, blood
sticky under our feet, the skulls of their children
smashed in our holy crusade.

No one escaped the justice of our God.
    I am David, I am mighty,
    and behold, the Lord is with me.

I took Michal, daughter of Saul,
to be my wife and lover;
I took Abigail, a widow,
to be my wife and lover;
and then Ahinoam
to be my wife and lover;
then Maacah and Abital
and Haggith and Eglah,
to be my wives and lovers—
and concubines without number.
But when I saw Bathsheba, no one
could satisfy me till I had her.
So, being king, I had her,
and murdered her faithful husband. Then
our gloomy local prophet
said unto me, "Thou art David,
and God hath put away
thy sin." In a tumult
of joy I smashed and burned
the ancient city of Rabbah
and made slaves and concubines
of all its godless people
who live without the blessings
of the law.
    I am David, I am mighty,
    and behold, the Lord is with me.

Now the waves of death are upon me,
and I call upon the Lord:
the foundations of heaven move,
and smoke streams from His nostrils.
He thunders from the heavens
and rewards me much, according
to my righteousness, for
I have kept the laws of God.
He hath made all my ways to be perfect.
    I am David, I was mighty,
      and behold, the lord is with me.

JONAH

You remember the old story,
a fisherman bragging about the one
that got away: "This big," he says,
"*this big* it was, you never saw such a fish."
"No," says the other guy, "and neither did you."
It was that kind of day—on the run
from God, I stowed away
on the S.S. *Tarshish*, got
dry-heave sick in a wicked wind,
dreaded for hours the creaky tub
would sink the lot of us, finally
got flung overboard by panicky sailors
like so much ballast, and then,
after all that, to see this monster
come bearing down on me like I was
breakfast—oh,
you can see why I've been a little fuzzy
ever since. Was I really inside—
like people are saying now—I mean
really inside that fish, or whale,
or whatever it was—every eyewitness
gives you a different story—anyway,
was I *really*
in the belly of that thing
for three whole days?

I know what you're thinking—
"If you don't know, who does?" That's
what you're thinking, isn't it? Well,

don't get smug, this
is stickier than you think.
You've had those days, don't tell me you haven't—
you brush the cobwebs out of your eyes,
cursing the sunrise,
and there's that big jug
sitting there empty, and you say, my God,
did I drink it all? And the truth is,
you don't remember. It's like that.
I do remember this big mouth coming at me
like a tidal wave, and the next thing I know
it's three days later, and I'm on the beach,
hungry as a seagull and ready to kill
for a mug of the good stuff. But
what exactly had happened?

I know there's this rumor going around
that I was inside that fish, but wait
a minute, look at my skin—
all in one piece. How
could I have been swallowed and not been
chewed up, or at least munched on a little? Or
suppose I did somehow get gulped down whole,
and didn't break my neck going through
that churning gullet, then
what did I do for air for three days,
down there with all those squid and dead herring?
Just try to picture that scene,
as I do all the time now—
swimming in belly-soup, seasick whenever
the beast does its foraging dance,

and when it cranks up its digestive machine,
the squid and I get sprayed
with acid strong enough
to eat away my sandals.
And maybe the whale, or whatever it was,
gets lucky, hits a school
of irresistible tidbits,
and all of a sudden I'm dumped on by a ton
of fresh mackerel.
Am I supposed to believe
I survived all that for three days
and three nights, the gristly stomach
grinding away at everything inside,
squeezing me to mush? Oh,
come on!

Look, if you're so crazy
about the fish story, I've got a lot
of others you'd like—maybe
the one where Moses' staff turns into a snake,
or the time he splits the Red Sea like an apple,
or when Joshua knocks down a stone wall
by yelling at it,
or when Samson kills a thousand armed men
with a piece of bone—say,
I could go on and on. And if
you swear to me you swallow all that,
I mean really absolutely believe it
at high noon on a sunny summer day,
then maybe I'll think again about
swallowing the whale.

MARY

Years later it was, after everything
got hazy in my head—those buzzing flies,
the gossips, graybeards, hustling evangelists—
they wanted facts, they said,
but what they were really after
was miracles.
Miracles, imagine! I was only a girl
when it happened, Joseph
acting edgy and claiming
it wasn't his baby . . .

Anyway, years later
they wanted miracles, like the big-time cults
up in Rome and Athens, God
come down in a shower of coins,
a sexy swan, something like that.
But no, there was only
one wild-eyed man at our kitchen window
telling me I'm lucky.
And pregnant.
I said, "Talk sense, mister, it's got to be
the one thing or the other."
No big swans, no golden coins
in that grubby mule-and-donkey village. Still,
they wanted miracles,
and what could I tell them? He
was my baby, after all, I washed
his little bum, was I

supposed to think I was wiping
God Almighty?

But they *wanted miracles*, kept after me
to come up with one: "This fellow at the window,
did he by any chance have wings?"
"Wings! Do frogs have wings?
Do camels fly?"
They thought it over. "Cherubim," they said,
"may walk the earth like men
and work their wonders."
I laughed in their hairy faces. No
cherub, that guy! But
they wouldn't quit—fanatics, like
the gang *he* fell in with years ago,
all goading him till he began to believe
in quick cures and faith-healing,
just like the cranks in Jerusalem, every
phony in town speaking in tongues
and handling snakes. Not exactly
what you'd want for your son, is it?
I tried to warn him, but he just says,
"I must be about my father's business."
"Fine," I say, "I'll buy you a new
hammer." But nothing could stop him, already
hooked on the crowds, the hosannas,
the thrill of needling the bureaucrats.
Holier than thou, he got, roughing up
the rabbis even. Every night
I cried myself to sleep—my son,
my baby boy . . .

You know how it all turned out, the crunch
of those awful spikes,
the spear in his side, the whole town watching,
home-town folks come down from Nazareth
with a strange gleam in their eyes. Then later on
the grave robbers, the hucksters, the imposters all
claiming to be him. I was sick
for a year, his bloody image
blurring the sunlight.

And now they want miracles, God
at my maidenhead, sex without sin.
"Go home," I tell them, "back to your libraries,
read about your fancy Greeks,
and come up with something amazing, if you
    must."

Me, I'm just a small-town woman,
a carpenter's wife, Jewish mother, nothing
special. But listen,
whenever I told my boy a fairy tale,
I let him know it was a fairy tale.
Go, all of you, and do likewise.

JUDAS

Ask Peter, ask Paul—the really unbearable part
was figuring out those hillbilly parables
We understood the straight stuff, "Blessed
are the peacemakers," and such, but not
those constant "It is like unto's . . ."
They always sent shivers through us—we knew
there'd be catechism after the sermon.
"It is like unto sowing seeds," he'd say
in that Nazarene country drawl,
"some of them fall on good soil,
others on rock." Well, everybody knows that,
but what did he mean by it?
He'd only say, "Who hath ears to hear,
let him hear." Big help.
Or he'd say, "It is like unto a mustard seed
that grows into a huge plant." Mmm-hmm.
He'd say, "The kingdom of heaven
is like unto leaven," and so on.
And then, of course, that inevitable
"Who hath ears to hear," etcetera.
We were always as nervous as cats in a doghouse,
John sneaking glances at James, James
dragging his toe in the sand and looking
at Thomas, Thomas looking doubtful,
all of us hoping that someone would understand.
But we never did, not one single time—finally
he always had to explain. "The *field*
is the *world*," he'd say, his eyebrows grim

as a tax collector, "The good seed
are the children of the kingdom, get it?"
Oh, sure, it's easy when you already
know the answer, but
suppose it'd been you, hearing
for the hundredth time
those words like needles in your nerves,
"It is like unto, it is like unto . . ."
It drives you over the edge, finally, even
Peter claiming he didn't know him,
and I . . . Well,
with or without those thirty pieces of silver,
it's a wonder that none of the others
crossed him first.

JESUS

We're cast in the image of God,
they say, but
up here the image blurs—
that Pharisee at the edge of the crowd,
the one with a burro's belly
and a toad's complexion
is he the real thing, God
in the flesh?
Or maybe that saintly starveling, all
bones in her pinched piety—does God
have a profile like hers?

Just days ago, these very faces,
rainbowed with joy, saw palm trees
ripped and strewn for the son of man. Now
my palms are red,
and it's all changed—bloodlust
smudges the thousand grins
of God. Here
in this Friday frenzy, just
look at them, the veins
in that legionnaire's legs, the brutal
mouth, the pocked face, and . . .
And of course the handsome boy out there
eyeing the splendid line
of that girl's arm—them, too.
It all counts,
doesn't it?

I suppose they aren't even wondering,
this godly rabble out for fun,
expecting something big today, something
spectacular. So I should be telling them,
now, before I'm dust forever—
you don't pay off an ugly squint
with a nice ankle; a luscious
lower lip doesn't make up
for a running sore; and above all, nobody
ever promised you justice.
All you have to know is
that a beautiful shoulder is God, but
a twisted leg is God, too,
and crooked noses and bad teeth. This
is the real revelation—that God
is only a trick with mirrors, our
dark reflection in a glass.

So up here, getting this panoramic view,
I hear the voices of God on every side,
all mocking me, "Hold on,
it's your big scene!" And I cry out
to every smooth and sacred cheek,
to every holy wart and pustule—the spikes
tearing at my hands—I call to every
body on this hill of skulls,
    Why?
    Why have you
    forsaken me?

III.

THE HOLY MEN

THE FAITH-HEALER SPEAKS

The laying-on of hands: faith
that could move these barren hills
pulses through our fingertips,
and Darwin's demon apes of hell
howl the name of blasphemy.
We cast them out—yea, and the Serpent
who deceiveth the world, that
whoredom sitting on the waters,
with whom the kings of earth
have committed fornication, our faith
will cast it out! For so it was
by that little creek in Tennessee,
three hundred of the faithful come
marching to Zion in the August sun,
to pray above our crippled brother
seven raptured hours, and sing
    All hail the power of Jesus' name
till every hill in Tennessee
believed; and sisters in the throng, adrift
in all that heat and joy, fainting for love
of the Lord, and men with muscles like the rocks
in God's good earth
watered the weeds with tears;
and when at last our hands came down
and touched those withered legs,
the afflicted brother stared around
with eyes that rolled with the love
of Jesus—and slowly rose, *rose,*

till he was on his knees,
our hymns still ringing off the hills:
   My faith looks up to Thee—
and then, in the heavenly current
coursing through our fingers, that
chosen man
set his teeth and rose again
rose upright, in a tide of holy pain,
to stand on his own feet—stood there
a minute by the clock, before he slid
to grass! Praises, then, our praises rang
across the state of Tennessee—
for the Lord healeth those that are broken, He
telleth the number of the stars
and calleth them by their names—oh, Lord,
ravish our hearts with love
in the perfume of Thine ointments, in honey
and milk, in the savor
of saffron and pomegranates, come
to us now, Lord, come
as You did that sunny day in Tennessee—
come to us now as You came
to the halt and lame, to the woman
blind with cataracts, five hours in prayer, all
the faithful on that hilltop
shouting love to heaven, till
the demon shrieked aloud
and she was Saved, staring
into the sun till her dead eyes found
visions, omens crawling in the sky
that no one else in all that throng could see.

For so it has been, too,
here in the City of Angels, Zion of the West,
home of our Tabernacle, borne
from Tennessee, to fight
the poison plagues of Darwin on
the shores of this great ocean—here too
we have touched the fevered and palsied, here
we have said to the blind and bent:
"Thy faith hath made thee whole."
This boy, now,
fair and virginal, undefiled by woman, yet
possessed by the demon called
in the Godless clinic, "diabetes"—
this child was Saved,
as clear as Jesus' Word, washed
in the blood of the Lamb, as ready
for heaven as earth—the boy
had prayed with us, and his father
prayed, until their faith grew strong; and
here in these browning hills, we gathered
the faithful in our hundreds, chanting
till sunset:
 Praise God from Whom all blessings flow—
and the father, in that hour of triumph,
tears of good tidings on his cheeks,
called above the chanting,
"Come out of the boy, thou unclean spirit!"
And at that cry of victory,
he threw away the pills, those ugly
relics of his doubt—
and the boy cried out, rejoicing!

But oh, ye children of the light—
what terrors after sunset, in the hours
when Satan stalks the heathen dark
wherein the beasts of the forest move,
when Darwin's monkeys squeal their dirty lust,
and lions roaring after their prey do seek
the meat of God. The boy
had schooled with infidels, his faith
was thin like his youth, not robust
like his father's manly Grace—after two nights
the child would not breathe as he should,
his tongue went thick, perverse. Seven
of the faithful stayed always
and chanted at his bed till dawn, and he waxed
stronger for a moment here, a minute there—
then wavered, waned, refused to sing the hymns.
"*Father*," he whispered,
in a voice that spoke the spells of midnight,
"*Father, give me the pills*"—and we heard the Serpent
slithering among us: the smell
of evil filled the room. Air! Light! We rushed
the boy in blankets to the hills
and faced him to the rising sun, and chanted,

> *Nearer, my God, to thee . . .*

"Give me the pills," he whispered. But
his father's faith held strong; he cradled
the small head in his arms and sang,

> *Holy, holy, holy, Lord God Almighty!*
> *Early in the morning our song shall rise to Thee!*

By the third verse, morning smog
had shut off the sun,
and in the swirling mist the demon rose,
Darwin's great beast rose before us,
scarlet with abominations—Satan
passed his hand over the boy's
sick faith: cold
settled in his limbs.

Oh, Lord,
Thou art Alpha and Omega, beginning and end,
and what is man, that Thou art mindful of him?

But yet he is not dead—the boy
only sleeps in the Lord. Tomorrow
he will rise again, our strength
will quicken his, the father's
sainthood will cast out this demon, Death,
and the boy will wake: here, on this
same hill, here in the sun in the City of Angels,
a thousand of the faithful sing from dawn
to sunset, praising the bountiful Lord,
and tomorrow we shall command this child to rise
and glorify God on earth, his body whole and strong,
his faith healed by the laying-on of hands,
the abiding prayer: tomorrow, yes,
tomorrow *he will rise.*

A PRIEST FOREVER

The first time?
So long ago—that brown-eyed boy . . .
How can I say this, Your Reverences,
so you'll understand? Maybe
it was the tilt of his pretty neck
when he pondered the mysteries—Grace,
the Trinity—the way his lower lip
curled like a petal, the way . . .
But you know what I mean—down
from your high pulpits and into the dirty streets—
you know there are some provocations
the good Lord made no sinew
strong enough to resist. Think
of David and Jonathan, snarled forever
in a tender web as tough as twine—
like that, maybe—like being driven
by flames, deep in the places we hide,
renounce, deny . . .

No, Monsignor, try to understand—
if your inquest here is meant
to "evaluate" me again, then
you have to feel that fever in the loins
when a child's face looks up
from the wafer-thin body of Christ, innocent eyes
flooding with wonder. You have to see
that the Lord, the good Lord,
has willed something beyond commandments,

beyond dogma, beyond law or custom,
something—irresistible . . .

All right—the first time—
of course I remember.
It was a smoldering August afternoon,
the hottest day in the history
of this whole state. And there
in the cobweb aftermath
of too many questions—what is mortal Sin?
what are the dangers to chastity?—alone,
almost alone in the church, after
my little pupils had all run off
to baseball, ice cream, whatever,
he lingered on, in the dim vestry . . .

Well, if you insist, I did ask him
to stay—because,
after all those catechism lessons, there was
one urgent question hanging
in the clammy air,
and inch by inch, among the ghostly chasubles,
we found ourselves edging closer to it.
Somehow, then, my anointed hand was blessing
his brown hair, one finger ordained to touch
the petal of that lower lip. And there
in that sweaty room—dear Jesus, how I still
feel the heat—I . . . We . . .

Yes, of course—the others. All
the others . . . But after the first time,
how do you tell them apart?
Let's see—there was a blue-eyed kid
with an angel's tongue—what was his name?
And a cherub with golden hair, who
used his indifference like a tease. And . . .
Sixty-eight of them, did you say? All
testifying to . . .

What? I? "Ruined their lives"?
Wait a minute, let's get this straight—
my passion *gave* them a life, gave them
something rich and ripe in their green youth,
something to measure all intimate flesh against,
forever. After that,
they ruined their own lives, maybe.
But with me they were full of a love
firmer than anything their meager years
had ever tasted . . .

Love, you heard me—you
with all your degrees, your tight mouths,
your clinical jargon, don't tell me
you've never had a movement below your belt
that wasn't intestinal. Listen,
this is not in Aquinas,
not in our learned encyclicals. But
there's a force that moves in our marrow,
that slithered there, long before

theology—something with ape in it,
something with the squirm of snakes,
the thrust of rams. And whatever it is,
it knows what it wants . . .

Ah—your glittering eyes
show me you understand. And your ramrod backs
tell me you'll never admit it.
But I'm not alone here, am I?
We're in this together, the same old
celibate fix—"It's better
to marry than to burn," our little
inside joke. And it all comes down
to one poor sinner in a straight-back chair
entertaining a dozen sanctimonious . . .

That word is for the record, Monsignor.
Remember the last time we met like this—
how I pleaded time, place, circumstance,
mitigating niceties, anything but the truth.
And how you enjoyed flaying me then—
you nailed me to lust like a rugged cross,
brushed aside my passion, turned your back
on my word made flesh, hoping
that no more boyish voices
would speak its name to daylight . . .

Yes, Reverends, I learned
a little something then, in all that
groveling—learned that whatever

the meek may wangle in this life,
whatever skimpy joy they manage
to snuggle up to at night, one thing
is as certain as graveyards—the meek
will never, in any shy season,
inherit the earth.
So excuse me if I don't
bob and duck this time.
You have your job to do, go ahead,
throw me to the wolves
and pay off my little lovers—
plaintiffs, have it your way—
hush them up with a million bucks
in widows' pennies. Not a bad price
for all that ecstasy . . .

Oh, I know where I'm headed—
to "therapy," as we always say,
a little paid vacation
with others who loved not wisely
but too young—and also, of course,
with the usual slew of dehydrating
whiskey priests. But don't forget
that when they say I'm "recovered" again,
they'll send me off to another parish,
with more of those little lambs—a priest,
after all, is a priest forever.
Meanwhile, as I bide my time,
and count my beads, and hum to myself
those luscious songs of Solomon,

what I'll be thinking about—
rely on this, Your Reverences—
what I'll be thinking about
is that brown-eyed boy
with the graceful neck, and the lower lip
that curled like a petal.

THE TELEVANGELIST THINKS IT OVER

The rage of that mighty organ, the glare of the
    floodlights,
the rush of the congregation's *Holy, Holy*—then
the pinpoint spot and the hot red eye
of the camera zooming in—who could resist
that adrenaline, the director's end-of-the-world
countdown—three, two, one, *you're on*—
and the slimy serpent Satan
trembled again as the Good Book
whipped above my head
and the Apostle's voice, a silver trumpet, cried,
    Have faith, and doubt not!
And believers called out,
from their gray desperation, Amen! Amen!

And you, whoever—wherever you are,
you would have felt the same,
and done the same as I, if your face had smiled
for years on the Salvation Network,
your joyful noise racing along
the airwaves, bringing in
all those cards and letters: the sick and shut-ins
bribing eternity, blessing our mission,
mailing in payments on a mansion
in our Father's house . . .

And you, yes, even you would have tasted
honey in the mouths of the faithful

as they pressed your hands and embraced you
with holy fervor, would have felt
that tug-of-war between loins and loyalty, as
the maidens in your flock, those little lambs
came to you in the darkest hours
to minister to your needs
    thou hast ravished my heart with thine eyes . . .
you too would have felt called
to bless them with a laying-on of hands
as they shed their robes—
    thou art all fair, my love . . .
you too would have cherished caresses
as velvety as money in your fingers
    open to me, my love,
    for thy thighs are like jewels . . .
the feel of it all so succulent
it was indeed the Word made flesh,
a taste of heaven itself—and all the while
the payments on heaven gushed in,
rivers in the promised land
flowing milk and honey, and we smiled,
and smiled, and crushed the Serpent under our heel,
and raised the beams of our gleaming cathedral
and the golden baths of our earthly mansion,
and still the maidens came for comfort,
and our bankers battened in Basel and Bimini,
and all the world was sunshine.

But
the slithering Snake would not stay down

on his filthy belly,
reared up on human legs to speak
scandal to the servants of Mammon,
reviling us in their godless courtrooms,
dirtying all our sunshine
with their shadows, warping our charity
into crimes—"Embezzlement!" "Adultery!"
dragging our piety through
the gutters of the pagan press—
and Pontius Pilate, in his midnight robes,
crucified us on cold steel bars,
and humiliation wracked us to
the breaking point
    for oppression maketh a wise man mad . . .
but we kept, for spite, a smiling face
    have faith, and doubt not . . .
to mask a bitter heart
    O the laughter of fools is a crackling of thorns . . .
until at last, at last, the festering
was salved, the iron gates flung open—and now
once again we walk triumphant through
these smutty streets, smiling—but
our faithful followers no longer turn
the other cheek, they curse our enemies
    for now is the time of the vengeance of the Lord . . .
and they reach for the hem of our garments,
to be in touch with God,
and once again our organ calls to sinners,
and the fierce red eye of the camera
sanctifies our every move

as we speak in tongues and bruise the Serpent,
  for in faith all things are possible . . .
and in our righteous anger now we scourge
with whips of hellfire all those blasphemers
who worm their monkeys into the seed of Adam,
we scourge the harpies who slaughter our innocent
    babes,
we scourge all men who defile other men,
and we scourge false prophets who prattle
  "reason"—
for the only light that truly saves is faith,
and everything denied to us by reason
is given by the Lord—so the righteous seek out
miracles,
    miracles,
      miracles
to redeem their dreary lives—
and we smile, and smile,
and say to all of them, *have faith.*
And doubt not.

REVEREND EUPHEMISM
ADMONISHES THE SKEPTICS

You secular humanists say it's a "War
Of Religion," but that's just impertinence:
This isn't "Religious Warfare,"
It's only Sectarian Violence.

You atheists only seem interested in
Something that you can revile, hence
You babble "Religious Warfare"
When it's only Sectarian Violence.

It's true we kill thousands of heathens, because
They're infidels in the most vile sense—
But don't say "Religious Warfare"
When it's only Sectarian Violence.

READING THE HEADLINES

Lusty priests paw kids in dusty Texas.
In floral Florida, where love goes oral,
Preachers grope the organs of their organists.
Oh, why can't pious people just be moral?

In Maine a pastor snitches widows' pennies,
In court his *mea culpa* is pathetic.
Church trustees embezzle from the many.
Oh, why do pious people have no ethics?

In Brooklyn rabbis can't disguise their *Greed*,
In Georgia, *Envy* causes priests to quarrel,
In Tehran, mullahs' *Wrath* makes many bleed.
Oh, why can't pious people just be moral?

Religious people have their explanation, and
They don't *need* morals like, say, you and me,
For Protestants elect "Predestination," and
When Catholics mouth Hail Mary's, they're home
     free.

AND THEN THE
PERFECT TRUTH OF HATRED

There was a preacher in our town
whose Sunday text was the Prince of Peace,
but
when he looked out at the Monday world—
at the uppity blacks and pushy Jews
and sassy wives and sneaky heathen—blood
scalded his face as purple as if
he'd hung by his heels. Then
his back-yard, barber-shop, street-corner sermons
scorched us with all the omens of siege:
our roofs aflame, tigers at the gates,
hoodlums pillaging homes, ravaging
wives and daughters, the sky
come crashing down,
and we gazed into his blazing truth
of Onward Christian Soldiers,
A Mighty Fortress Is Our God,
Soldiers of the Cross. No question now
of sissy charity, this
was the Church Militant, burning
its lightning bolts across
our low horizons.

It's been a while since that preacher went off
To the big apartheid in the sky,
and the only hint of eternal life
is the way he resurrects each week

to sell salvation on the screen.
He's younger after all these years,
in designer suits and toothy smiles,
but we know him by the cunning eyes
where he harbors his old stooges,
Satan, Jehovah. He calls them up,
and across the country, glands begin
pumping bile into our lives:
sleet storms in the voice,
cords in the neck like bullwhips,
broken promises, broken bones,
the wreckage of his deep
sincerity.

IV.

LIVING WITH
THE BIBLE

GERTRUDE

Gertrude Appleman, 1901-1976

God is all-knowing, all-present, and almighty
—A Catechism of Christian Doctrine

I wish that all the people
who peddle God
could watch my mother die:
could see the skin and
gristle weighing only
seventy-nine, every stubborn
pound of flesh a small
death.

I wish the people who peddle God
could see her young,
lovely in gardens and
beautiful in kitchens, and could watch
the hand of God slowly
twisting her knees and fingers
till they gnarled and knotted, settling in
for thirty years of pain.

I wish the people who peddle God
could see the lightning
of His cancer stabbing
her, that small frame
tensing at every shock,
her sweet contralto scratchy with

the lord's infection: *Philip,*
I want to die.

I wish I had them gathered round,
those preachers, popes, rabbis,
imams, priests—every
pious shill on Gods payroll—and I
would pull the sheets from my mother's brittle
    body,
and they would fall on their knees at her bedside
to be forgiven all their
faith.

MARTHA

Martha Haberkorn, 1899–1983

Imagine her moving from sink to stove,
from need to need,
planting seeds, baking cakes,
visiting shut-ins,
and on Sundays glittering
with stained glass, hearing always
the praises of a jealous God,
and every night His fierce voice
hissing, "Listen, listen,
    a fire is kindled in mine anger
    and shall burn unto the lowest hell,
    and sinners shall be devoured
    with burning heat and with bitter destruction,
    the teeth of beasts, the poison of serpents,
    the sword without, and terror within,
    to Me belongeth vengeance."
Thus
spake the Lord.

So when the bad times came to her troubled mind
and she bore the modern torture of her pills
and the ancient menace of the lake of fire,
and every night came on in a black torment,
then the Lord was faithful to her bed,
reminding her in the dangerous hours
of all the evil things she'd ever done—
the omissions, the white lies, the private

secrets locked away—little
derelictions from
her eighty-four years of goodness.
And God would not relent
when her body trembled
and her words came in gargling
whispers—when, in the dark chambers
of the heart, the pounding
was hammers on nerve-ends—the sword without,
the terror within—and a tiny voice
grieved her guilty life:
"I've done so many bad things, and now
Jesus won't forgive me, the Lord
won't let me rest."

How can we then forgive this God
who will not forgive His saints?
We are here to witness
that the sins of the Lord are past pardon.
He is therefore banished from our planet
to shuffle through a universe of stars,
while the tree of knowledge sows its golden apples
all across this land.

ALIVE

Uncle Jimmie had a hunch that cancer,
the rat that gnawed away behind his ears,
was part of the warm earth and silver woods
and snowy meadows in the mountains. Surgeons
stabbed at the rat: scalpels sliced away
the ears one April dawn, as catbirds,
perched in the morning treetops, mocked the
  calling
of cardinals. Stabbed and missed—the rat survived.
The day they clipped out Uncle Jimmie's cheeks
and upper lip, he pondered artichokes,
truffles, and a certain Tuscan wine.
And when they snipped his nose, he wept for roses
and the fresh sea breeze—and thought a while, and
  played
his hunch: *Stop cutting*, Jimmie told them, *let
me go to earth and snow and silver trees.*

But the rat kept gnawing, and Auntie Flo went on
reading St. Paul (*The works of the flesh are
  uncleanness*),
and praying, and paying the bills—and the sur-
  geons huddled,
frowning at Jimmie's want of reverence
for faith and modern medicine. With skillful
suturing, they lifted out his tongue
and dropped the wagging muscle in a pail,
and Uncle Jim, who used to murmur quatrains

out of Omar, kept his peace. Still, his eyes
kept pleading: *Stop the cutting, let me go
to earth and silver trees!* But Jimmie knew
the rat would work in just behind his eyes,
and Auntie Flo would go on reading Paul
(*They that are Christ's have crucified the flesh*)
and praying, and paying the bills—and the pale
    blue eyes
would have to go: one Sunday after Angelus, Jim
    began
his dark forgetting of the green
wheat fields, red hills in the sun,
and how the clouds drive storms across the sea.
Some Monday following, a specialist
trimmed away one-quarter of his brain
and left no last gray memory of Omar
or snowy fields or earth or silver trees.
But Uncle Jimmie lives: the rat lies quiet now,
and tubes lead in and out of Jimmie's veins
and vents. Auntie Flo comes every day
to read to bandages the Word Made Flesh,
and pray, and pay the bills, and watch with
    Jimmie,
whittled down like a dry stick, but living:
the heart, in its maze of tubes, pumps on,
while catbirds mock the calling of cardinals,
artichokes grow dusty green in sunshine,
butterflies dally with the roses,
and Uncle Jimmie is no part of these.

CREDO

I am modern. And educated. And reasonable.
And I believe in Jesus Christ, son
of the living God.
When they tell me He
was born of a virgin, I say, well,
it's unusual, of course, but in the arms of God,
anything is possible . . .
When they tell me that a bright new star
appeared in the eastern sky,
shining over His manger, I say, well,
I know it's not customary
to improvise stars like that, but remember,
we set up searchlights now, just
to open a used-car lot, and after all,
this *is* the Son of God, isn't it? . . .
They tell me He cast out demons,
and I say, well,
you have to understand the peculiar idiom
of a given historical time . . .
They tell me his voice could calm a tempest,
and I reflect on all the unexplained
phenomena
of our physical world . . .
They tell me His touch cured blindness,
made the lame walk, the lepers clean,
and brought corpses back to life—
and I'm reminded of the psychic component
of so much modern medicine . . .

They tell me He fed five thousand
with five loaves and two fishes,
that He walked on the surface of the sea,
that He rose from the dead—
and I relish the poetic truth
of those venerable symbols.

In the backward villages of Asia,
the gods have as many limbs
as spiders, and take on monstrous forms
as quickly as a cloud. The natives,
shrouded in their age-old ignorance
and superstition, believe
the most bizarre tales about them,
despite the best efforts
of our enlightened missionaries.

PARABLE OF THE ONE-TRACK MIND

The Book of Jeremiah:

"Thou hast polluted the land with thy whoredoms and with thy wickedness . . . thou hadst a whore's forehead, thou refusedst to be ashamed."

The Book of Ezekiel:

"They committed whoredoms in Egypt; they committed whoredoms in their youth: there . . . they bruised the teats of their virginity."

The Book of Hosea:

"Go, take unto thee a wife of whoredoms and children of whoredoms: for the land hath committed great whoredom."

The Book of Isaiah:

"The Lord will visit Tyre, and she . . . shall commit fornication with all the kingdoms of the world."

The Book of Amos:

"Thy wife shall be an harlot in the city . . . and thou shalt die in a polluted land."

The Book of Joel:

"They have cast lots for my people; and have given a boy for an harlot, and sold a girl for wine, that they might drink."

The Book of Revelation:

"I will shew unto thee the judgment of the great whore that sitteth upon many waters:

With whom the kings of the earth have committed fornication, and inhabitants of the earth have been made drunk with the wine of her fornication . . .

And the woman was arrayed in purple and scarlet colour, and decked with gold and precious stones and pearls, having a golden cup in her hand full of abominations and filthiness of her fornications:

And upon her forehead was a name written,

MYSTERY, BABYLON THE GREAT, THE MOTHER OF HARLOTS AND ABOMINA-TIONS OF THE EARTH."

Exegesis # 1:

"Whosoever looketh on a woman to lust after her hath committed adultery with her already in his heart."

Exegesis # 2:

"He that goeth about as a talebearer revealeth secrets."

PARABLE OF THE
PERFIDIOUS PROVERBS

How better it is to get wisdom than gold.
Money buys prophets and teachers, poems and
art,
So listen, if you're so rich, why aren't you
smart?

He that spareth his rod hateth his son.
That line gives you a perfect way of testing
Your inner feelings about child molesting.

He that maketh haste to be rich shall not be innocent.
But here at the parish we don't find it overly hard
To accept his dirty cash or credit card.

Hope deferred maketh the heart sick.
That's just why the good Lord made it
mandatory
To eat your heart out down in Purgatory.

Wisdom is better than rubies.
Among the jeweled bishops and other boobies
It's also a whole lot rarer than rubies.

He that trusteth in his own heart is a fool.
Trusting your heart may not be awfully bright,
But trusting Proverbs is an idiot's delight.

THE DOCTOR-KILLER READS HIS BIBLE

The defendant's attorney argued that the killing of those who performed abortions was "consistent with biblical truth."
—*New York Times*, Nov. 1, 1994

It is written:

"The Lord God is
a consuming fire,
eye for eye,
tooth for tooth,
burning for burning;
so cast out devils,
kill every woman
who has known a man,
stone her with stones
that she might die . . ."

for it is written:

"Thou shalt not suffer
a witch to live,
beware of men
defiled of women,
destroy young and old
with the edge of the sword,
scorch them with fire
    (serpents among you,
    bad seed)

the sword to slay,
dogs to tear,
beasts of the field
to devour and destroy,
and let the dead
bury the dead . . ."

for it is written:

"There shall be wailing
and gnashing of teeth,
famine and plague,
generations of vipers,
locusts and scorpions,
fathers shall eat
their sons, sons
shall eat their fathers,
bad seed,
strike them,
destroy them utterly,
show no mercy,
carcasses falling
like dung on the field . . .

All these things
the Lord has spoken:
fear the Lord
and obey, for *it
is written.*"

GRAVITY

*F = Gmm'/r2: directly proportional to the
product of the masses, inversely proportional to
the square of the distance . . .*

One false step and you're off the ladder,
plunging in free-fall   through
a lifetime   proportional
to the product of its losses   down
through decades to Mother Earth   who breaks
your heart   your spirit   your bones
jarring your life into ceaseless   pain.

And the pain that will not stop
is a poison vine, its roots deep in your chest,
is a snake reaming your veins, gouging out endless
yesterdays, the ceaseless pain
of history: night after night
you cannot sleep—in the dreary hours
you read about the Age of Faith,
when godly ones bowed to a holy
ghost, told their beads to a blessed mother,
and ripped off the screaming fingernails
of unbelievers; when priests, inspired
by the Pope's own personal blessing,
tore off nipples with red-hot tongs;
when monks thumbed out the eyeballs
of heretics and saints, and seared their flesh
to purify their souls.

With enough gravity and pain,
with enough pain long enough,
we will see their glowing eyes: the fervent ones
on the march again. But because our memories
are inversely proportional to
the distance between them, we don't recall
that when the high wall between priest
and politics is wrecked by frenzied mobs
screaming Hallelujah,
then the godly ones will lead us again—
our ears sliced off,
our tongues cut through,
our foreheads branded—
they will lead us triumphantly back,
back through our hazy memories,
to burn again
in an Age of Faith.

AN EYE FOR AN EYE

"Are you saved?" he asks me,
sunrise in the corner of his eye,
a snag at the edge of his voice.
In a blur of memory, I see the others:
the preacher who used to trounce my tender sins,
kids at church camp, their brimstone choirs
shrill with teenage lust gone underground,
true believers come knocking to tell me
that flaming hell is real.
And those twisted faces on the tube:
Christian gunmen in Beirut, their hot eyes
exploding in the beds of sleeping children;
the righteous hatreds of Belfast, lighting
Irish eyes like a tenement fire;
the eyes of the Ayatollah, squinting with joy
at the blood of his blindfolded prisoners.
It smolders in the windows of the soul,
that holy blaze, never so bright
as in human sacrifice,
never so proud as in crimson crusades,
the glorious, godlike destruction.

A SIMPLE EXPLANATION
FOR EVERYTHING

When the Syrians came down like a wolf on the fold,
Ahab of Israel sharpened his sword,
And soon the Jordan was running with blood.
    Why did they kill?
    They killed for the Lord.

When Muhammed ran off to Medina, he swore
He would roar back to Mecca, this time with a horde
Of warriors thirsting for infidel gore.
    Why did they kill?
    They killed for the Lord.

When the Pope's Inquisition put thousands in chains,
Their bodies were broken and branded and gored,
And the innocent perished in spasms of pain.
    Why did they kill?
    They killed for the Lord.

When Puritans filled all New England with dread,
Hunting down women whose thoughts they abhorred,
They strung up the witches until they were dead.
    Why did they kill?
    They killed for the Lord.

Now our Born-Agains tell us God gives them the word:
Send infidels off to their blazing reward!
So far-away rivers are running with blood.

Why are we killing?
We kill for the Lord.

FLEAS

I form the light, and create darkness:
I make peace, and create evil:
I the Lord do all these things.

—Isaiah, 45:7

I think that I shall never see
a poem as ugly as a flea,
a flea whose hungry mouth is pressed
against a buttock or a breast,
a flea that spreads disease all day
and lifts its little claws to prey:
poems are made by you and me,
but only God can make a flea.

I think that no one ever made
a poem as powerful as AIDS,
or plagues that may in summer kill
half the bishops in Brazil
and share the good Lord's Final Answer
with clots and cholera and cancer—
for God concocted pox to mock us,
staph and syph and streptococcus:
poems are made by bards or hacks,
but only God makes cardiacs.

I think that I shall never smell
a poem as pungent as a hell,
where grinning devils turn the screws

on saintly Sikhs and upright Jews,
giving them the holy scorcher,
timeless, transcendental torture:
poems can make you want to yell,
but only God can give you hell.

LAST-MINUTE MESSAGE
FOR A TIME CAPSULE

I have to tell you this, whoever you are:
that on one summer morning here, the ocean
pounded in on tumbledown breakers,
a south wind, bustling along the shore,
whipped the froth into little rainbows,
and a reckless gull swept down the beach
as if to fly were everything it needed.
I thought of your hovering saucers,
looking for clues, and I wanted to write this down,
so it wouldn't be lost forever—
that once upon a time we had
meadows here, and astonishing things,
swans and frogs and luna moths
and blue skies that could stagger your heart.
We could have had them still,
and welcomed you to earth, but
we also had the righteous ones
who worshiped the True Faith, and Holy War.
When you go home to your shining galaxy,
say that what you learned
from this dead and barren place is
to beware the righteous ones.

V.

SALVATION

CHECKMATE

God is all-knowing and all-powerful.
　　　—The Baltimore Catechism

. . . and the Lord hath taken away.
　　　　　　—Job, I:21

Busy as you were, God,
when you were alive,
you always found time
to torment the woman I love—not just
that old kid stuff, her tonsil
-ectomy,
append
-ectomy,
those casual tweaks, your afternoon's
amusement—no,
I mean the really dirty tricks, the mast
-ectomy,
blighting her beautiful body,
and then of course her hyster
-ectomy,
the doomed flesh gouged away
just as you pre-ordained,
and listen, God, I haven't forgiven you
her hacksawed knees, those twin
-ectomies,
nor am I overlooking
your other little favors:

her tricky heart, thinning bones,
lazy glands—and when you gave her
your best shot, that sneaky stroke,
you thought it'd be Strike
Three, right? Well,
not on your life, big boy,
she's tougher than you thought,
and now that you're dead,
she's dancing on your grave.

GATHERING AT THE RIVER

Is it
crossing over Jordan
to a city of light, archangels
ceaselessly trumpeting over
the heavenly choirs: perpetual Vivaldi,
jasper and endless topaz and amethyst,
the Sistine ceiling seven days a week,
the everlasting smirk
of perfection?

Is it
the river Styx,
darkness made visible, fire
that never stops: endless murder
too merciless to kill,
massacres on an endless loop,
the same old victims always
coming back for more?

Or is it the silky muck
of Wabash and Maumee, the skirr
and skim of blackbirds,
fields of Queen Anne's lace
and bumblebees? Well,
go out once more, and feel
the crumble of dry loam,
fingers and soil slowly becoming
the same truth: there in the hand

is our kinship with oak, our bloodline
to cattle. Imagine,
not eons of boredom or pain,
but honest earth-to-earth;
and when our bodies rise again,
they will be wildflowers, then rabbits,
then wolves, singing a perfect love
to the beautiful, meaningless moon.

BUT THE DAISIES WILL NOT BE DECEIVED BY THE GODS

Seductions as countless as crosses,
as icons, none of it ever
surprising, not even
the stare of the sky
keeping score. The prize for yielding,
for giving in to paradise,
is laying down the awful burden
of mind: surrender
rings from the steeples and calls
from the minarets and temples.
But challenges sing
in the sway of treetops,
in the flutter of sparrows,
in chirring and stalking,
in waking and ripening—let
there be light enough, and
everywhere backbone stiffens
in saplings and clover. Praises, then,
to sunfish and squirrels,
blessings to bugs. Turning our backs
on the bloody altars,
we cherish each other, living here
in this brave world
with our neighbors, the earthworms,
and our old friends, the ferns
and the daisies.

ABOUT THE AUTHOR

Philip Appleman has published eight volumes of poetry, including *New and Selected Poems, 1956-1996* (University of Arkansas Press, 1996); three novels, including *Apes and Angels* (Putnam, 1989); and half a dozen nonfiction books, including the widely used Norton Critical Edition, *Darwin*, and the Norton Critical Edition of Malthus's *Essay on Population*. His poetry and fiction have won many awards, including a fellowship in poetry from the National Endowment for the Arts, the Castagnola Award from the Poetry Society of America, the Friend of Darwin Award from the National Center for Science Education, and the Humanist Arts Award of the American Humanist Association, and have appeared in scores of publications, including *Harper's Magazine, Nation, New Republic, New York Times, Paris Review, Partisan Review, Poetry, Sewanee Review*, and *Yale Review*. He has given readings of his poetry at the Library of Congress, the Guggenheim Museum, the Huntington Library, and many universities. Appleman is Distinguished Professor Emeritus at Indiana University; a founding member of the Poets Advisory Committee of Poets House, New York; a former member of the governing board of the Poetry Society of America; and a member of the Academy of American Poets, PEN American Center, Poets & Writers, Inc., and the Authors Guild of America.